OX

DATE DUE

GAYLORD			PRINTED IN U.S.A.

DEC 2 1 2007

Ox

Christopher Patton

SIGNAL EDITIONS IS AN IMPRINT OF VÉHICULE PRESS

Published with the generous assistance of The Canada Council for the Arts
and the Book Publishing Industry Development Program of the Department
of Canadian Heritage.

SIGNAL EDITIONS EDITOR: CARMINE STARNINO

Cover design: David Drummond
Photo of author: Juergen Raeuber
Set in Minion by Simon Garamond
Printed by Marquis Book Printing Inc.

LIBRARY AND ARCHIVES CANADA CATALOGUING IN PUBLICATION DATA

Patton, Christopher
Ox / Christopher Patton
Poems.
ISBN 1-55065-233-0
1. Title.

PS8631.A848O96 2007   C811'.6   C2007-900560-8

Published by Véhicule Press, Montréal, Québec, Canada
www.vehiculepress.com

Distributed in Canada by LitDistCo
www.litdistco.ca

Distributed in the U.S. by Independent Publishers Group
www.ipgbook.com

Printed in Canada

for my parents

Contents

~

Acknowledgements

Grateful acknowledgement is made to the following publications, in which some of these poems first appeared, often in somewhat different form:

The Antioch Review: "Leaf Bee"
Ducky: "Weed Flower Mind" (excerpts)
Emergency Almanac: "Bird Seed," "Cloud Hold," "Fire King"
The New Quarterly: "Poisoned," "Seed"
The Paris Review: "Red Maple," "Quaking Aspen," "Weeping Willow," "White Pine," "Hawthorn," "Beech," "Doe's Bones," "Stone Gate," "Graft," "Leaf," "Sheaf," "Wine," "Hale," "Lull," "The Vine Maple"
Western Humanities Review: "Weed Flower Mind" (excerpts)

The first section of *Ox* received *The Paris Review*'s Bernard F. Conners Prize for Poetry. "Red Maple," "Doe's Bones," "The Vine Maple," and excerpts from "Weed Flower Mind" were reprinted in *The New Canon: An Anthology of Canadian Poetry* (Véhicule Press).

The author would like to thank The Canada Council for the Arts for Creative Writing and Travel Grants. Residencies at Yaddo, The MacDowell Colony, the Virginia Center for the Creative Arts, the Djerassi Resident Artists Program, and the Millay Colony for the Arts were also invaluable.

My thanks as well to Richard Howard, Lucie Brock-Broido, Alice Quinn, Bruce Beasley, Stephanie Bolster, Sally Dawidoff, Barbara Nickel, Elise Partridge, Julie Rose, Beth Thomas, Richard Wertime, and Carmine Starnino for their insightful critiques and kind encouragement.

In the pastures of the world
I endlessly push aside tall grasses
in search of the ox.
Following unnamed rivers,
lost on the interpenetrating paths of distant mountains,
strength failing, vitality exhausted,
I cannot find the ox.
I only hear locusts chirring through the forests at night.

—K'uo-an Shih-yuan

I

RED MAPLE

Acer rubrum

Four plates of raw
iron, folded over one
    another, found there was no
        way to hold the world.
        The world did not mind;

turning, it looked
as a child would, to itself,
    and found new life in the muck
        a mare's hooves made
        as she stamped and cried.

When the plates split,
`a foal descends, and her pain
    is not everything it
        knows: the leggy
        cluster prancing

    under cirrus
celebrates an awkwardness—
    honour to the universe
        the hole I came from
        sends forth to eat.

Wobble-legs falls.
Gets up, different. Its red-green
    flower: adders' tongues, flawed
        trumpets, baby-
        squalls of flower-birds:

the spring wind shakes
it through ten thousand forms,
    forms falling through themselves like
        a train station
        departure board's

    >

rain of changes.
Foal grows then, knows harness.
    Being tightens to one thing
        and another—
        and when the train comes,

    its works are done.
Lying lightly on the grey
    mud of the old carriage road,
      or pressed by boot
      soles into the mud,

    confetti, red
paper for a celebration:
    a branch coughs in the wind,
      the flowers give
      up their attachments.

QUAKING ASPEN

Populus tremuloides

    A hand brushes back
the wet hair to slick. It stands in
    tufts. There's something he lacks,
        bedraggled tom, sad boy
        on the boardwalk, catkin
    in the rain, dangling and bored.
    A breeze blows him near

    an hourglass figure topped
in a scrappy display of styles—
    the pistil's scarlet
        tendrils sway, the way
        a movie star's hair sways
    when a man she has spurned
    grabs her, and she turns.

    They enter open arms.
On ribbon leafstalks pivot
    in another's breath till comes
        his spray of pollen dust—
        well, then things go slack. The rest
    going on without, he leaves,
    dreams of waves and waves

    in the wind. Turns on lights,
dresses, goes back down to the shore,
    just hanging. Sees a boat
        rising on a green sea
        churned by wind and light to foam,
    leaf-foam where the water
    lifts ships to shatter—

the cliffs he meets are
ruin to him she shifts around
    to live. She goes where
        sailors are, and the dives
            they seek her in will take them
    deep. Next morning the waves
    wash boys up in coves,

    and walking on the shore
littered with spent flower-shells,
    an old woman finds more
        fallen than she can count.
            One in her hand, she tongues
    a sugary matter
    at the mouth's corner.

WEEPING WILLOW

Salix babylonica

Colourless on the green
but visible in relief—
   hair-thin parallel veins
      course out from a silver crease
      towards the leaf-edge
   obliquely: old men
   who've forsaken
their power to do otherwise.

The leaves swaddle a wet
nub. It swells and tries to slip
   between. The leaves, jaws, part
      around a cleft-tipped tongue that now
      should splay to calyx—
   but willow knows
   how the wind blows
and wraps her daughters up in down.

Tonight they will gather,
once more, to hear of the great
   sorrow she has suffered.
      There was a time—there was a time.
      The old queen, searching
   for her pendant, scans
   the water, pendent,
a rack of broken necklaces,

   while the chastened buds push
through the leaves, towards the light.
   Small flowers emerge to blush.
      They hang heads shyly, their silky
      hair woven over
   and under in braids.
   Even though buried
sometimes, the strands are ongoing

that the wind climbs, bearing
pollen up the shifting ropes
    like a lover scaling
        a wall towards erect, unpetalled,
        downturned flowers.
    When he arrives, they
    stare lustlessly.
What we do has been done before.

WHITE PINE

Pinus strobus

1.

    Hands that ache for home will break
ground, as a covenant. When the plough
        of stars that leads the settlers west
        by night through the sea-mess
            vanishes, a foam-lipped mouth
            starts to open beneath
            the prow. Wind and rain, lost for weeks. When
            pine-pollen drifts
like smoke over the face of the water,
raining brimstone on the pioneers' oak decks, they quake
    before the shore's green-lashed lock, and open
    it, and deal with the Indians

    for a near-white light-weight wood
that will be carved with equal
        ease in all directions: fascia mould-
        ings, panellings of old
            colonial interiors, fan-
            lights, ornaments fan-
            tastical, bobsleds, hobbyhorses—even the San-
to Domingo heavy elegant
mahogany furniture comes from white pine, traded
    on the Guinea Coast for men, men taken
    across the sea for sugar cane . . .

2.

A green brush moving down
a brown field, browsing, each fine-
            needled cluster finds its direction
            through variation;
                        some fall like tufts of lion fur
                        to the forest floor
                        and redden, a resting place for the glance that fears
moving up the grown trunk's furrowed brow—
up to the waving twig-tips, papery pale brown nubs,
            amphora-shaped, fertile yet formal, as
            gold-gilt minarets in Is-

            lamabad. Most were cut or burned
for farmland, but the bared land
            wasn't easily broken, and the stony
            uneven soil has grown
                        new species in. And on a rise
                        no one knows who owns
                        grows a stand that escaped, distant-intimate as jazz
to the painter passing a beech tree's
old codfish-flesh-yellow leaves strung out on wires; he sees
            a sudden miracle of clarity
            in infinite variety:

            bowing under the crystal gaze
of borne-up mica-glinting
            April snow, a pine-lion-sapling
            thrives, and to the leaning
                        cement-mixer in an oiled
                        stream, a flaking failed
                        cow-of-rust's front quarters, and to the painter tied
to his mast, from which it sounds like sirens,
says, Animal of mineral, rest. Open the eye's
            painted window, and wind will clear the heart
            of dust. Thou art that, that thou art.

HAWTHORN

Crataegus intricata

A soldier, reflecting
in a ditch, saw through his tears
    what the water's mirror
    warned. No river
will bear me away—I squat
steeped in myself. And *you* have crouched
    so long beside me, staring, that now
        no one will grasp you: your open
        arms have filled with thorns.

    His wood wrist clenches.
His eyes close. Muddied thoughts form
    between the furrowed bones
    the tip of a horn.
It lengthens—rusty cockspur,
medic's bloodied needle, dull sword
    turned but not transformed to a ploughshare
    with which he tills thin soil. Guarding
    the dull green bud

    that comes, father blares
blood-red alarms, though his war
    is over. Rose, a cousin,
    visits, but not often.
After she has cleaned and cooked
for them, she spreads a lurid whorl,
    then full, seeding hips; when he invokes
    a military rationale,
    she slams her farewell.

Later the crops wither.
He finds them work down the road,
     and directs: stiff, assured,
     we are here to guard
the flowering dogwood, whorish
in underthings, beneath the limp-
     wristed red maples, who make you blush.
       Don't touch us!—now stand in this hedge,
     and show your courage.

     Bud unfurls—a thumb's whorl
testing thé air, pressing it
       cautiously, as a blade.
       Leaves his father's side,
     hitches, steals clothes and fruit, works
some strange shifts, until a woman
       enters his arms. Thrown into the thick
       of it, he shows her how the heart
       that was hurt, will hurt.

BEECH

Fagus grandifolia

A thought made of wind,
touching matter, taking the shrivelled forms
of last year's leaves. Stationed around the bud
    in gilt silver braces,
        the browning frames congeal
    to guttering flames in a dark
          scriptorium—flames over
        the shoulder of a young scholar
    who wants to open himself
as a man does a book.

Downstairs, a girl cooks,
dreamily crumbling a core of garlic
—as if it were a cock she held between
    finger and thumb—to yield
        masses of substanceless
    paper, and just a little fruit.
          One hand fools with her skirt while
        the other crumbles. She smiles
    intricately, as she
seasons the scholar's meat.

He forgets the root.
The bud, a swelling taper collapsing
in the boy's avid hands, gives up translucent
    outer scales with ease.
        What he sees reassures,
    and then it becomes unsettling,
          the pages grow more opaque
        as he goes on, the act
    intensifies to a point
until there is nothing

in him of meaning—
just leaf-paste scattered in a flowerless hollow
where senile flames rasp and clap in the wind.
    The book left open
        he leaves: out through the gate,
    into the woods, towards the grave
            where his mother was laid
            in an old beech tree's shade.
        He traces, on that unbound page,
    the heart he would forgive.

POISONED

1.

    honey the laurel flowers
form. On a hillside grave they grow alone.
A soul floats, with a bee's seeming
    drowse, to the opening clusters
     of hot-pink, five-plated flowers—
      when it has poised to sip,
      a spring-cocked filament, tripped,
       scatters pollen
        over the abdomen.

2.

    A bee moves with a lone soul's
ease: like a pendulum unhinged undulates
back to the hive. And it will hurt, as
    a flame hurts the edge of a chart
    of shoals, when one who was apart
      comes to fill his prison's
      paper hexagons
       with nectar the cells
       will hold, though it kills.

II

LEAF BEE

1.

 —I am not that I am,
you know that.
    —What's the matter.
        —Nothing's
the matter.

2.

   —Why can't you sleep.
       —I woke
 from a dream of reason. I saw
  a yellow leg caked in
  white pollen and knew

 I was not meant to be
this way.
   —Not meant to be what way.
—I will show you. I will make a scene
 of it.

3.

  A mother and a son
 in parts.
   An old warped door,
 sorrow, blows open,

we are in a kitchen.
—Come here then. Why can't you just leave
me be?
      (—I am home. I should know not
    to go there . . . this is how it goes
      when I do. I know how
        to cut it out.)
                —You

are an impossible
pest today. Now what's the matter?
—Nothing. Nothing is the matter now.
   —Cut it out then.
                (—I will show you
    a life . . . but not this life.

4.

    This is not my life.)

BIRD SEED

—I am late. Private.
Complacent. Past condition.
(—Her voice.)
     —Morning. Sunlight. Coffee
back on the deck watching life
at a feeder. Nothing is left
 by noon but commotion

 of new leaf, a bold
new white note:

     I am enough
I am—enough

     well no—not yet
 not that

    in light is joy
in life

   this love is one this way

He comes back and he laughs.

 —Another day off?
—Sits there and fidgets. A door
slams behind him and then

      leave be?
 be loved! beloved

    It seems . . .
there's nothing to fear, it's just, I'm
 a week late now.
     —I'm sure

it's nothing at all.
—Hear the birds at it?

                         a son
a sign a seed

            he doesn't hear
      them at all

            we lit we left

they mean we have my love a gift
      to open and open

DOE'S BONES

—A sunlit lot. Clearcut.
Slash smoulders. Crabs of a beer-
coloured grass. A torn-up midden heap,
its tiny lustreless bits
of oyster shell. One lady-thin
translucent alluvial fan

of scallop. A doe gone
off to moss, snake-work of back,
a scatter of ribs.
Dear bones. I hate
that I love. What have I done?
(A blank slate, he said. But I can't!
I told him—this is what I want.)

No answer. A lichen
antlers cut alder.
I move
heavily downslope through fern and thorn
toward a shore. An ocean
throwing ocean up. This is it
to give life? a plume of white spit,

bark scraps knocked up and dropped
on shore rocks—and now a raw
red sawn face. Sea-worn log end-on. Dread
uneven drum.
Well. How apt.
It has been more or less a war
to get here. And here is so far.

CLOUD HOLD

—White boats   absolute
dissolute   one moors at another
    for water   it wants to hurt
no one and won't   well, I want to
say I've been going through
    some things   I don't know how to start

    such beautiful boats!
all are needed   none forsaken   one
    wet and light   one white and grey
one close to witness   I am new
to this ease   not to know
    then to know!   look, I found a way

    across old water
damage music to a shore beyond
    confusion   a sky all done
with cloud and clear   I want to have
more of you or none   crave
    me or leave alone   I went on

    the way through some things
of ours   invitations   a white dress
    I wore over fields breathless
beside you   all holes   yes I said
I do   I do   I did

STONE GATE

I let it go. Waves throw back
      white bodies and ivy twines
    in hollow trunks on slopes
    green above black ocean.
A rose climbs out of rock. A shape
      spreads in the shade of an oak

above heaped rock and crumbles.
       A wall gives. A leaf wanders through
    the shade of an oak. Stones
    are thrown one by one to
the heart of what they bordered on.
      A white moth disassembles

itself. Red ants pull it off.
      They come to know of me in bits.
    I am, and am weary
    of, beauty.
            —I think it's
time!
     —Yes, it is time, as they say;
     as if she has had enough.

You break, rose, up through a crack
      in the rock. Though you look and glance
    away, you may forget
    about flowering once
only. I am you. I am not
      you. There is no death. Speak! Speak!

　　　—O tempestuous.
Sugar bread. Sweet crab. What
ever is the matter?
　　　　　　　　—A wet
　　hiss. A red kiss. I am less
and less of what . . . I am not
　　what I was or will. I happen.

　　I have caught. O white
note. O hot weight.
　　　　　　　　　—I thought I knew.
I thought I would just *know*. You
　　are more than I would have thought
　　I could.
　　　　　　—I got up. I was full
of light and shade and grew

aware. I wanted to look
　　down the hall and went, and turned
away, and could not speak.
　　(What would one say? "I burn
to be"?) A coal shifted and broke;
　　I went in to look. I was all

　　I saw. I got up and went down
　　the hall. *That* is how
I am. A bit of weather.
　　　　　　　　　—I
　　thought I would know—I don't know
how one *could*. You are my
one yes. You are my own eyes.

UNDERWOOD

1.

    Rust pastoral!
A burned-out house upslope. Dark beams
drip on loose stove coils; pots and pans;
    a broken clock in a cracked clawfoot
        tub; the water runs it through. Poor
        clepsydra. A hair tucked behind an ear
            absently as she lifts from the blackened
            crib a burning child; he makes no sound,
        she's nothing more to fear.

2.

    A haunt of char
and air: to live and move under wood
where nothing left of her is not
    soot in a state of continual
        atonement. A grin of lettered key
        and earth (most are lost as the rest slowly
            fall to rust) jars and narrates all. Return
            it says to the scene. Return! Return!
    It will not let me be.

III

GRAFT

I

    A woman may wear
gold along her arms and rivers
    of gold meander
        down her sides and learn
           new ways to flow each time she turns
    and sighs on a couch. Or may dream
herself a fly immured
    in amber, awake far from home

    in a frightful state,
stroking an amber pendant
    between her perfumed
        breasts. Stroked to a charge
        amber draws up dried leaves and chaff;
    carved in human effigy
I have known it to
    sell for more than a man in the prime of life.

II

    Gold from shafts in hills
will gild the palm of a god
    or a tedious official.
        Rivers redirected
        fifty leagues by aqueduct
    rinse the ore in channels, filling
our jewel boxes with rings
    of a pure, ill-gotten yellow.

III

An eye is opened
in a tree by paring away
    the bark—a second
        twig slipped in—sap
        seeps from the slit, a well-shaped
    tear that hardens, as the tree bends
under a weight it can
        not foreswear, nor understand.

LEAF

In a poor man's field
sun spurs the dirt
to fecundity: a shoot
    nudges aside a sod and unfurls a weak flag.
      Caesar comes to see. And fails
      to see that though he wheels
    dirt beds around, chasing
the sun with his sweet peppers, when they darken
with a warm and spreading red,
    they do not blush at his command.

    This food needs no fire,
although a fire,
implicit, invisible,
    inaudible, flares in the apple on a branch
      out of reach, in the pear
      we slice in half and stare
    into, and in the useless
windfall too, spilt from a tree, bruised, its skin split,
flesh collapsing in wet pleats:
    a seed dries, hardens, sinks, descends

    through grass, stone, and dirt;
dwells there; and bursts
open to head for a half-
    remembered light. Resurrected. In a ritual
      way I store sorb apples in clay
      pots with broken floors to bury
    upside-down, two feet deep
in a sunny spot. He does not know the soil's
benediction, who chases
    fabled birds beyond the river
    Phasis: awfully precious,
they are dangled from heaven as playthings.

SHEAF

I

A nightingale pours
forth song, grave, sharp
notes broken or prolonged
    from a branch, quavering with a selfless
        joy. Two chicks
        beside him cock
    their heads, strive to repeat what they hear,
and learn, by nature, what we
    earn by art and squander.

With a finger I
have traced the hands
of poets, orators,
    senators who applauded Cicero's
        rictus in
        the Forum; when
    I labour to rework what they wrought
for the ages, I think what
    they thought, and now cannot.

II

Alexandria!
A king who heard
of paper there and thought
    to raise for thought a great erection
        set one on a spit
        of land that years of silt
    have borne back round now to shore: a dike
that keeps from the sea a flat,
    insipid, brackish lake.

WINE

. . . the infant who resolved
  at Saguntum to climb
  back to his mother's womb:
  that place burned that year, at the hands of Hannibal.

 Lacking this
end to endless
appetite I
  fill a glass, my tremulous
  hand unable to hold the over-
flowing vessel: a glass
   within whose swirling forms
   a formal banquet room—
  I see red veins on the cheeks of Caesar:

 on that map
the weak, thin wine
of empire spreads
  as his wife takes her bath for hours
  in the milk of half a thousand asses.
Serving unspeakable thirst
   the hand at the nipple
   the finger on the rim
  plead . . .

HALE

The sun sheds
light on sleeping slave
girl and wakeful
  Caesar alike. On their shoulders
    it warms them as they walk
    towards a rock
  in the heat, where he starts
to shake uncontrollably.

For his seizures,
the lights of a hare
with myrrh, or else
  horse piss mixed with smithy water
    fresh from a forge whose arms
    have not harmed
  their bearers. A star's position
causes flesh commotion:

in the lost
Colossus of the Sun
at Rhodes, I poked
  my head into shattered limbs
    wherever I found a rift:
    the sunlight's shafts
  and intangible columns all
day made animate the dust.

LULL

I

     Now the lion by law
weds the lamb. The lamb
dies, an eagle eats
    its eyes. Brownish seed-maned grasses poke through the jaws.
       Tossed naked and weeping
       into the world, knowing
nothing but hurt, growing hurtful, we learn
to make our children swaddling clothes of the beasts
       we catch in woven
       hunting nets. It's not by malice but love
     skewed that their souls
     are forged into toils.

     When scythes have slit the wheat,
the flax stalks are cut,
and for the coats to steep
    and loosen, are plunged in a vat and sunk with weights;
       hung and turned head downward
       in the sun, they dry, and dry
are beaten with a tow mallet on stone;
the worst are combed with iron hatchels for lamp wicks,
       the best carefully
       groomed into nets so fine, one man can carry
     enough to harvest
     an entire forest.

II

We have formed a cloth
incombustible,
a "live linen" woven
    of asbestos. Wrapped around a trunk, it will mute both
        axe and echo. A napkin
        made of the stuff, stained
with spreading archipelagos of wine,
was thrown once in the banquet's blaze, and we, amazed,
        ceased a drunken song
        when after some seconds it rose on tongs
    more white and pure
    than thought could endure.

III

A monarch's corpse will wear
a shroud of live linen
to keep his ashes
    apart from the ashes of the pyre. Though there are
        places which are always on fire,
        in 79, admired,
admiral of the fleet at Misenum,
I first thought the plume rising from Vesuvius
        harmless, a pine headed
        heavenward. When the soldiers at the foot sent for help
    my light, steady
    vessel was readied—

but the sea roiled with debris
at Retina, we
could not land. "Fortune
    favours the brave," I said, "conduct me to Pomponianus."
        At Stabiae, across the bay,
        I found my friend afraid.
To make calm, I bathed and dined with him, then dozed
as the courtyard filled with cinders and pumice stones.

The building, rocking, woke me.
We walked to the ships, protecting our heads
with pillows tied on.
Stones rained and ruined.

IV

The lion paws the dirt
when about to die,
and roars—kingly
investigating rolling wheels on an empty chariot,
the vultures overhead, he fears
but does not flee the flame
that paints his pelt in gold. As his gaze rules
grasses without deceit, as he lets no glance inward
remain oblique,
so did I, carrying a torch into the smoke,
form a third eye
and consent to die.

On a sea too boisterous
to set out upon,
the ships rose and keeled.
We boarded to wait. I lay down on a sail and asked Marcus
for water. When the air fumed
with sulphur (the smoke plume
had seemed a pine tree and was falling on us)
I asked for more. When the others had fled
through the brown and yellow
air, I tried to rise, and fell, and felt
come upon me
an uncommon calm.

becomes an image
of what it fears: beneath the conifers,
    leaves arrayed in parallel sun-angling planes that flare
    gold in such deep shade or
brandish fire-engine reds as fires rage
in fall on open slopes; spreads through regions moist to wet, clear-
cuts often, and lava flows; wants either courage

    or rain. Sites on fire
are later favoured by Douglas fir, from whose needles
    the gold-nubbed chanterelles poke with their undulating
    gills; beneath whose flutings
of ridged, rough, mud-brown bark the wood, admired
by rained-on Coast Salish as fine fuel, even as it threw
    troublesome sparks, seeped a pitch that soothed wounds and
    tempered spears,

    salmon weirs and fire
tongs. Thin green bracts emerge from under
    scales on every cone, three-forked slips like the feet and tails
    of hiding mice who've failed
in some small quest. (Bees, droning their beware
nearby, hoard from black cottonwoods a sticky balsamic
    anti-infectant resin, and one unlucky mouse has mired

    in the hive.) The Great
Spirit gave to the Salish redcedar
    to honour a man always helping others. Tree
    of Life with scale-like leaves
  overlapping in a woman's long plait.
The bark made clothes, the wood became their dugout canoes
    and bailers, combs, fishing floats, cradles, coffins, spirit

      whistles and berry-
drying racks. Above, below the cedar
            whose kindness is such that a stranger needing strength
            need only stand beneath
      with her back to the trunk, my landlady,
a lawyer, half-Déné, from the porch pours rainwater out
      of our old beer bottles. It is enough to see clearly.

SEED

1.

A seed is a sound.
    Shhhhh! Shhhh. It's like a robe the air wore
    open. Brushing grass on a berry-
        hunt for mother and the brother-baby, out
           hours, I am son in the sun. O brash. I fill
           the yellow plastic ice-cream pail to spill
      over in a grass lap. Then munch. A touch of rash—
      make it stop. Shhhh. Shhhhhh.
    Fast run to the centre of care.
    There is no one there.

2.

Talk, sticks of seedstalk:
    years in the weed-field, your arms trapped
    in t-shirts, inside-out, half-off. Fingertips
        brushed by a wind that lives and dies, and dry,
           stiff-walled seedpods rattling. A seed makes a sound
           in its sheath, it can make a wound
      no one would believe. Shhhh. Come, sit here near the heat.
      Flames in his flesh-sheets.
    Liar in lair, I feel no fear.
    I am feel-no-fear.

IV

WEED FLOWER MIND

1.

A nature no one could tell you how to tend.
Brown stalk and cracked pod. Spilt milk, blown seed.
A waste of pain. A leaf-tooth
gnawing the edge of noon. —In the yellow
swaying heart-waste of August, an unearthed shout;
buttercup at ankles, towers of white sweet
clover, scent of yarrow
from overhacked, eroded bluffs; nameless, homeless, weed-mind

2.

on ditch-verge, lawn edge, mound of mine-waste,
roadside, in wet low place, on rock-slope, in untilled
field, in untold feel,
breeds and breathes; scythe and seethe.
Weed-leaves hiding leaf-faces. . . . Dawn zazen.
Monk stomachs grumble. Old grass and stone,
grind inside me; blithe
ash, black leaf, in fields of wild carrot where the goldenrod sprouts. . . .

3.

Can't inhabit this! the windows, burned-out
eyes, of abandoned brick warehouses;
floors, dirt, the root cracks. —Can't
inhibit it. —Snot and old weep
crusting on cheek, I quiver in a lit place,
a windless smoke; hard to stem; a white lace
heart, a blood spot I keep
blotting. I hit the road, as fall to the rutted dirt

4.

a few delinquent drops of rain. —A river:
rock-broken froth, moss-wet shelves, sinews
of unshelved water; a stale
recess; trembles, deeps; a caught
twig, shaken in bank-weeds, the current catches
at and lets go. Sit on the bank and watch.
—A roadside ditch: I squat.
The water smells of fever. I guess it comes from somewhere.

5.

I fear it never ceases. Vine-clasp, root-rend,
a piece loosed, its hold lost. I fall in with it
to drift on dark water
where a shade holds a bowl of ash in
its hands and blows. Silt rose. Incensed! Well, that's that.
—That's not that at all. (—It is so that.
Inches hid. What when.
Came un.) —You must go on, you know that. —I will offend:

6.

wind-raked weed-smoke: sour smoke, burnt brush in piles
off a bared hill: the smoke of what should not.
Mother pulls more out
and throws them on. God-sleight then,
god-sleight: walked weed-bloom and high brown grasses,
not happy, not sad, a seed, nameless, near-weightless,
as close to no body as body can
come. Ran far from, scorned tender. Came to fire, was fuel.

7.

And yet in gashes grew. In muck slough, on scree breast
of the steep slope. Each part kissed, each touched,
remembered life; forgotten
shapes flowered and burst, a root
sought entry, cracked rock-face; found shit-hole, ate toxin.
A face reddens. I *am* too much. Come gone love, come barren.
I guess it got, I shouldn't
have, hard. —A practice of ceaseless awareness. —No rest:

8.

haw-blocked, thorn-touched, steps retraced, a ditch crossed:
seeking the serene, mannered garden
I balk, hedge in my blood.
A block struck. We sit for a talk. A curled
frond, shaken in rain, yields to the storm
its blast, its shriek and blow; it knows a calm
to be. Drenched, whorled,
pushing aside boundless grasses in search of the ox. . . .

9.

Crow-tussle over corn stubble. And grasses
at edges: hair bentgrass, soft, nodding bluejoint,
timothy, meadow barley. . . .
(—Wheat, oats, barley, rice, rye.) —Oatgrass;
foxtail barley's fan of red-brown fur,
alert, at rest, at one. So is it here
I might atone for the mess
of fear I go on in. —Go on or go in. —The possible crosses:

10.

hoof-churned mud-flat by the creek, a stew
of shit, thistle, grass-tuft, muddy water
pooling in hoof-prints. Barbed seeds
in my socks, and burs. Barbed wire. A gate
on a field of dung-faced cows and calves I pull
shut to scan uneasily for the bull,
eyes bird-eye quick. —Bird-heart.
Your greed and fear, your good and your bad, entangle you.

11.

—Weed-snarl at woods-edge: I kneel. I list to small
promptings: daddy longlegs on a rock,
one leg cocked to the next
rock. Leaves shift, he leaves. Seemed safe
to tip, but the poured milk slops over the cup
lip to pool on unvarnished wood. He's up.
Not a good. Stalks off.
(What weeps.) I don't need this now! (Or me at all.)

12.

Untangle me. —You were no longer most.
You might admit now you were difficult.
—And meant to be. Please me.
Please, me. Plucked heal-all from graves,
loosestrife, nettles, oxeyes for her, all
by murder nourished: among etched, sensible
stones and dry wreaths shoves
the weed-bud, clenched, demanding, blind, impatient, fist

13.

through sleeve, head through hole, help me, no,
get lost! (Your leave of me. Touch not. Went angry
she.) In bank muck I find
an unfinished form, sobbing and rocking, is
it me or my lost one, we can't be sure,
will it live, will they call it a disaster,
a surging (—it is what is)
—barely permissible, always suppressible, never extinguished though,

14.

of vicious, noisome feelings, unprofitable graine
encombring good corne: darnel, onion grass,
crabgrass; surging, useless.
Untangle me. —Lost in the fallow,
you swing a rusted sickle and it takes you down.
But look, self-heal, heal-all. You are your own
poison. How can you
not see you are your own and only medicine.

15.

—Break. —Refrain. —Work: pulling weeds
from the gazebo stones: brown moss, yellow
wood sorrel; three small heart
leaves round a flower-bell are a bow,
two-in-one, one-in-two: in rain
they fold, paired hands, gassho. Or spread to the sun:
we open, yes, just so,
and what we need is not apart from what you need.

16.

I pick with my father: spilt arc of blackberry
brambles across a back-lane fence. False
chamomile in the cracked
pavement. Thorns, berries. Bees in the thorns.
Sails falling off white flowers. The bees shake
them loose as, for good, he wishes he could make
me his. This small forlorn
who does not know how to carry what the bees carry.

17.

A deadly nightshade edges that confusion.
It winds up in the holly behind his garden.
That green will clamber near
what's grown: sink of whiskers, the sweet
known of his scent, shower steam, the length of his
revelation as he towels. What size!
(And what might.) (No do not
go into that.) Gentle, don't go . . . good night, good night. . . .

18.

It opens and closes. His summer done. I'm home!
Tears at the door. They sting and run off. So what
comes next? Not sure. What now?
A touch, a cool remove. And now?
Not sure. What dies? What rules? What does she feel
I am? (—Yes but what else.) —Chamomile
tea, an autumn flu,
I curl in chills beside her, quilted and harmless, unarmed.

19.

Uncross and up. I loved my eyes. Now, awake,
stirred in sunshaft, dust foretells of light
and shadow: one bears it one
is borne. —Within light there is
darkness. Do not try to understand that
darkness. Do not grasp after the light.
Just walk. —Sticks clack. Robe sleeves
lift up and fill, grey sails, black sails . . . what stirs? who walks?

20.

who bears? what is born? I stood in a door too
late at night and watched what two-in-one
would do: weed-small on stone
threshold, wind-whipped, was thrashed, was far
and near while they rolled as summer winds will
roil in making light. Their glory ruled.
Next day, changed. You wear
me out! Maybe when it all comes off we'll do——

21.

Death-knell in a hole-wall. Rang the spade bell, two,
three, *chring* of rock in soil. Treeplanting.
Levered load up and bore
a bit to left; turned, heft fell.
Knelt to sleuth for a lost self. No self. A worm-
half laughed. Felt-soft burns in the leaf-halls. A form
falls away in a spall
of flame or will—I follow halting to—see it through—

22.

White walls of old bed sheets. A naked room.
A tongue-house. Stirring tongues of leaves. They sip
and slip. An odour of.
Mouth of leaf-flame. Shhhhh. Your mom's
not here. She shouldn't ever. I have nowhere
to. Come air. Come nowhere. Come nowhere. —So here
you are. —Here I am,
an empty room where he comes and goes—I am not him—

23.

The seed has flown. It falls to loose dirt. Down,
gone, sown. Forgotten. In woods, no such as weeds,
and the flesh, red mud, gives
way with ease to the shovel; holes open
at my feet for red oak, dogwood, white
birch, sweet gum: loose teeth I pack in. But look what
comes up: a weed-sprout, in hand,
trembles, snail-tendril, seed testes. Bladder campion?

24.

Touch-me-not? —Two bells. Rise slow. Walk.
—Sitting spent. Flowing in ditch-grass, a fresh
trickle now, where coltsfoot
lions pounce, and leafy new
ladders climb of blue, wet nipples: the return
of forget-me-not. I asked her to help me, she turned
away, I don't know how
to help you. (I turned away—I couldn't make . . .

25.

I couldn't take it.) Outside the garden grew
a dragon in my grain. Held high a steel shaft.
Ached with weight. Made maw.
Drove down again. To pry dirt wide
rocked back and forth. To sledge young cedar (rag-strips
of red bark, wet flap on wood) sharp the tip,
true the aim, then broad
the arc and down hard. Posts in, raise fence. Who knew

26.

he was already in and through? A panicked fire newt
darts through the weedage of my father's unused
plot: squash vines, rampant
parsley thickets, monkey weeds as children
we grew there from seeds. His wisteria blooms
a second time on the roof, modest in autumn,
he sells the house, moves down
the coast, remarries; who knows, he may have found a future

27.

to settle the past. Come gone love, come wisdom. Lost
in the holly, a beautiful weeping lady: deadly
nightshade, *solatrum*, soothing
painkiller; misreading turned her
solem atrum, black sun, eclipse: it
isn't half as poisonous as thought.
Bittersweet. The red berry
darkens and dries: doe eyes. Once more, the old mistrust,

28.

quivered, nervous. . . . Her gaze lifts and passes
above human things. Soon it is dinner.
My work is to prepare.
I walk out to the garden in a light rain
(the monastery needs it, too, a dry
August) and kneel in the bed (I don't know why
I am crying) where fawn
and doe, gone now, flicked their tails and browsed grass,

29.

and a web, abandoned, broken, gathers evening
between a mess of oatgrass and a fencepost:
slant stalks, turned tree, blast-place
of long-past. Stars of insect shells
and calls. They're all over. And now a verb-weed
opening: the noun-flower has gone mostly to seed:
to lose; to fail; to fall
head over heels into the earth where a rough unfastening

30.

power moves, wordless and generous, unknown;
to know it lives and moves. . . . Oh, enough.
Returning, early evening,
with ordinary gifts: carrots,
tomatoes, dill weed, sugar peas in a white
beat-up bucket. A step: I shift my weight
to test a flag we set
down this morning. Each stone a path. We are not our own.

Notes

Master K'uo-an was a twelfth-century Ch'an (Zen) master of the Lin-chi (Rinzai) school. The epigraph is his verse on the first of the ten *Ox-Herding Pictures*.

I

White Pine. "In the aboriginal American forest, [white pine] was perhaps the most abundant species almost throughout its range.... When the male flowers bloomed in these illimitable pineries, thousands of miles of forest aisle were swept with the golden smoke ... and great storms of pollen were swept from the primeval shores far out to sea." —Donald Culross Peattie, *A Natural History of Trees of Eastern and Central North America*. In colonial times, the British Navy cut white pine for mastwood.

Beech. "Our word *book* comes from the Anglo-Saxon *boc*, meaning a letter or character, which in turn derives from the Anglo-Saxon *beece*, for Beech." —Donald Culross Peattie.

Poisoned

Kalma latifolia, also known as "sheep laurel" or "lambkill." Audobon's *Field Guide to North American Trees*: "The leaves, which are poisonous to livestock, are seldom browsed. Honey from the flowers is believed to be poisonous."

II

Ovid, *Metamorphoses*.

Underwood

The clepsydra ("water-thief") was a Saxon water-clock. A bowl floated in a tub of water and sank as it filled through a small hole in the bottom. Lines on the inside of the bowl marked the passage of time.

III

The speaker throughout is Pliny the Elder. Phrases from his *Natural History*, sometimes adulterated, are used liberally in the first six poems.

Sheaf. Cicero was killed by bounty hunters in 43 BC as he fled to Greece. Mark Antony had his head placed on the rostrum in the Forum.

Hale. Caesar's seizures are my invention. The cure is recommended by Pliny. The Colossus of the Sun was destroyed by an earthquake before Pliny's birth.

Lull. A *toil* is a hunting net. The account of Pliny's death is based on a letter from Pliny the Younger (his nephew and adopted son) to Tacitus.

The Vine Maple. Pojar and Mackinnon, *Plants of Coastal British Columbia*.

IV

Zen Mountain Monastery, Mt. Tremper, New York. The stanza is Berryman's.

4.1–6 *Shikantaza* is the practice of "just sitting." "There is no attempt to develop concentration. . . . You simply watch the thoughts, the flow of thoughts, without analyzing them, judging them, attempting to understand or categorize them. You are just aware of them." John Daido Loori, *The Eight Gates of Zen*.

8.4 The *han* is a wooden block that hangs at the zendo entrance. A single blow announces that a dharma discourse is about to begin.

8.8 Adapted from Master K'uo-an's verse. The ox is a traditional figure for the true nature of the self.

14.4–8 Master Dogen said to the assembled monks:

Although there are a number of sages who try to study by cutting off the root of twining vines, they do not regard the cutting of twining vines with twining vines as "cutting." (*Katto.* Trans. by Mel Weitsman and Kazuaki Tanahashi, in *Moon in a Dewdrop*.)

"Twining vines," or *katto*, means wisteria, also its relative, kudzu. It can also be understood as "entanglements"—notions or attachments that hinder understanding. The sages of whom Dogen speaks have limited insight because they do not see that entanglements cut off entanglements. Elsewhere it is said that medicine and sickness heal each other.

14.6 "Self-heal" and "heal-all" are both names for *Prunella vulgaris*. It is further known as "sickle-wort" for the resemblance its flowers bear to that implement, and as "hook-heal" and "carpenter's herb" for its use, at one time, in the treatment of wounds inflicted by sharp-edged tools.

15.6 *Gassho*—a gesture of intimacy made by bringing one's hands together palm-to-palm.

19.4–7 Adapted from Master Shitou's *Identity of Relative and Absolute*.

19.7–8 Walking meditation, or *kinhin*.

27 Bittersweet nightshade (*Solanum dulcamara*), also called European bittersweet, and, according to Audobon's *Field Guide to North American Wildflowers*, sometimes deadly nightshade. Pojar and Mackinnon, however, reserve the name "deadly nightshade" for a different species, *Atropa belladonna*, which, they say, an old herbal, later mis-transcribed, describes as a *solatrum*.

Occasional phrases are lifted from old herbals and altered.

Signal
EDITIONS

Carmine Starnino, Editor
Michael Harris, Founding Editor

SELECTED POEMS David Solway
THE MULBERRY MEN David Solway
A SLOW LIGHT Ross Leckie
NIGHT LETTERS Bill Furey
COMPLICITY Susan Glickman
A NUN'S DIARY Ann Diamond
CAVALIER IN A ROUNDHEAD SCHOOL Errol MacDonald
VEILED COUNTRIES/LIVES Marie-Claire Blais (Translated by Michael Harris)
BLIND PAINTING Robert Melançon (Translated by Philip Stratford)
SMALL HORSES & INTIMATE BEASTS Michel Garneau
   (Translated by Robert McGee)
IN TRANSIT Michael Harris
THE FABULOUS DISGUISE OF OURSELVES Jan Conn
ASHBOURN John Reibetanz
THE POWER TO MOVE Susan Glickman
MAGELLAN'S CLOUDS Robert Allen
MODERN MARRIAGE David Solway
K. IN LOVE Don Coles
THE INVISIBLE MOON Carla Hartsfield
ALONG THE ROAD FROM EDEN George Ellenbogen
DUNINO Stephen Scobie
KINETIC MUSTACHE Arthur Clark
RUE SAINTE FAMILLE Charlotte Hussey
HENRY MOORE'S SHEEP Susan Glickman
SOUTH OF THE TUDO BEM CAFÉ Jan Conn
THE INVENTION OF HONEY Ricardo Sternberg
EVENINGS AT LOOSE ENDS Gérald Godin (Translated by Judith Cowan)
THE PROVING GROUNDS Rhea Tregebov
LITTLE BIRD Don Coles
HOMETOWN Laura Lush
FORTRESS OF CHAIRS Elisabeth Harvor
NEW & SELECTED POEMS Michael Harris
BEDROCK David Solway
TERRORIST LETTERS Ann Diamond
THE SIGNAL ANTHOLOGY Edited by Michael Harris
MURMUR OF THE STARS: SELECTED SHORTER POEMS Peter Dale Scott
WHAT DANTE DID WITH LOSS Jan Conn
MORNING WATCH John Reibetanz
JOY IS NOT MY PROFESSION Muhammad al-Maghut
   (Translated by John Asfour and Alison Burch)

WRESTLING WITH ANGELS: SELECTED POEMS Doug Beardsley
HIDE & SEEK Susan Glickman
MAPPING THE CHAOS Rhea Tregebov
FIRE NEVER SLEEPS Carla Hartsfield
THE RHINO GATE POEMS George Ellenbogen
SHADOW CABINET Richard Sanger
MAP OF DREAMS Ricardo Sternberg
THE NEW WORLD Carmine Starnino
THE LONG COLD GREEN EVENINGS OF SPRING Elisabeth Harvor
FAULT LINE Laura Lush
WHITE STONE: THE ALICE POEMS Stephanie Bolster
KEEP IT ALL Yves Boisvert (Translated by Judith Cowan)
THE GREEN ALEMBIC Louise Fabiani
THE ISLAND IN WINTER Terence Young
A TINKERS' PICNIC Peter Richardson
SARACEN ISLAND: THE POEMS OF ANDREAS KARAVIS David Solway
BEAUTIES ON MAD RIVER: SELECTED AND NEW POEMS Jan Conn
WIND AND ROOT Brent MacLaine
HISTORIES Andrew Steinmetz
ARABY Eric Ormsby
WORDS THAT WALK IN THE NIGHT Pierre Morency
    (Translated by Lissa Cowan and René Brisebois)
A PICNIC ON ICE: SELECTED POEMS Matthew Sweeney
HELIX: NEW AND SELECTED POEMS John Steffler
HERESIES: THE COMPLETE POEMS OF ANNE WILKINSON, 1924-1961
    Edited by Dean Irvine
CALLING HOME Richard Sanger
FIELDER'S CHOICE Elise Partridge
MERRYBEGOT Mary Dalton
MOUNTAIN TEA Peter Van Toorn
AN ABC OF BELLY WORK Peter Richardson
RUNNING IN PROSPECT CEMETERY Susan Glickman
MIRABEL Pierre Nepveu (Translated by Judith Cowan)
POSTSCRIPT Geoffrey Cook
STANDING WAVE Robert Allen
THERE, THERE Patrick Warner
HOW WE ALL SWIFTLY: THE FIRST SIX BOOKS Don Coles
THE NEW CANON: AN ANTHOLOGY OF CANADIAN POETRY
    Edited by Carmine Starnino
OUT TO DRY IN CAPE BRETON Anita Lahey
RED LEDGER Mary Dalton
REACHING FOR CLEAR David Solway
OX Christopher Patton

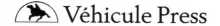 Véhicule Press

We hope this book will occupy a proud place in your library, and would appreciate your suggestions for reprints.

Title _____
How did you hear of this book? _____
Bought at _____ *or received as a gift* ☐.
Please send me a copy of the latest Godine catalogue and add my name to your mailing list for future catalogues.
I am particularly interested in: ☐ *Art & Architecture*
☐ *Photography*   ☐ *Fiction*
☐ *Typography & Graphic Arts*   ☐ *Children's Books*
☐ *Literature & Belles Lettres*   ☐ *History & Biography*
☐ *Gardening*   ☐ *Mysteries*
Name _____
Address _____
City _____ *State* _____ *Zip* _____
Please suggest another person who might like to receive Godine's catalogue:
Name _____
Address _____
City _____ *State* _____ *Zip* _____

Godine Books are available at your bookstore. Most bookstores will special order a title if they do not stock it. If you cannot obtain the book you want, you may order directly from Godine.

DAVID R. GODINE, PUBLISHER, INC.
306 *Dartmouth Street, Boston, Massachusetts* 02116

David R. Godine ~ Publisher
306 Dartmouth Street
Boston, Massachusetts 02116